1 Afternoon tea on the lawn at the
back of Hudson's Chemist Shop, High
Street, Eccleshall, *c.* 1900

2 At the throwing wheel at
Wedgwood's Etruria factory, 1870s

Victorian and Edwardian

STAFFORDSHIRE

from old photographs

Introduction and commentaries by

PAMELA MURRAY AND ROBERT FROST

B. T. BATSFORD LTD.

LONDON

ACKNOWLEDGEMENTS

The Authors and Publishers would like to thank the following for their help and for permission to reproduce the photographs in this book: Albion Galleries, 8/10 Albion Street, Hanley, 69, 75, 85; Mr Astbury, Oak Farm Holdings, 19 Watling St, Gailey, Staffs, 28, 32, 34; Owen Bennion & Son, Land and Estate Agents, 30 High Street, Eccleshall, 35, 89; Blakes Stationers, 55 The Strand, Longton, 16, 20, 68, 70, 71, 72; Mr C. L. Brightman, 40 Tithebarn Road, Stafford, 37; British Museum, 129; Central Reference Library, Birmingham (The Benjamin Stone Collection of Photographs), 6, 7, 26, 30, 48, 128, 134, 135, 136; Cheadle & Tean Times, Tape Street, Cheadle, 31, 59, 79, 87, 102, 116, 131; Mrs Chesters, Townhead, Foxt, Ipstones, 110; Miss C. Clarke, 78, Handsacre Crescent, Handsacre, Rugeley, 133; Mrs T. Davies, 11; Dudley Metropolitan Borough Library, 3 St James Road, Dudley, 60, 62, 65, 67, 80, 81, 82, 107, 109, 119; Mrs Evans, 133; Mrs J. Exton, Staffordshire County Record Office; Rev. D. Felix, St Paul's Vicarage, Heyburn Crescent, Burslem, 57; Mr Gates, Sheffield House, Longnor, 5, 91, 93, 94, 95, 96, 97, 99; Mr Gould, Townhead, Longnor, 92, 93, 94, 95, 96, 97, 99; Mr W. Groves, Pye Green Road, Cannock, 4; Trustees of Miss J. E. L. Harrison, deceased, 35, 89; Mr P. Harrison, Tanglewood, 200E Upper St John Street, Lichfield, 55; Mr J. S. Horne, 24 St John's Road, Rowley Park, Stafford, 9, 36, 46, 101, 120, 139; Miss I. Hudson, High Street, Eccleshall, 1, 21; Mr O. W. James, The Mackenzie School, Cheadle, 50, 58, 100, 103, 118; Miss D. Landor, Chadscroft, 43 Tithebarn Road, Rugeley, 27, 126; Mr A. Lawton, Wombourne, Miles Green, Bignall End, 15, 61, 106, 121; Mrs Mellor, c/o Longnor Junior School, 91; Midlands Electricity Board, 42, 43; Miss I. J. Morcom, Staffordshire County Record Office; Mr and Mrs Nadin, Yew Tree Cottage, Longnor, 98; Newcastle Museum and Art Gallery, The Brampton, Newcastle-under-Lyme, 44, 66, 140; Mr H. Parson, 'The Black Countryman', 64; Mr Robinson, Tithebarn Road, Stafford, 104; The Royal School, Wolverhampton, 53, 54; Rugeley Times, Bow Street, Rugeley (Mr A. W. Neal), 3, 8; Sandwell Public Library, West Bromwich, 64; Mr B. Sinkinson, Caprilla, 58 Cannock Road, Stafford, 47, 108, 113, 124, 132; Mr D. B. Slater, Hill Crest, Wincote Lane, Wootton, 112; Mrs R. J. Smith, 12 Lichfield Street, Rugeley, 8; Mr R. Speake, 74 Chester Road, Audley, 15, 51, 61, 84, 106, 121, 138; Staffordshire County Education Dept (Schools History Service), 12, 14, 18, 19, 23, 27, 41, 47, 52, 58, 64, 67, 86, 88, 90, 115, 119, 127; Staffordshire County Museum, Shugborough, 4, 29, 45, 53, 54, 55, 56, 91, 110, 114, 137; Staffordshire County Record Office, 25, 27, 35, 47, 57, 89, 108, 111, 113, 124, 130, 132; Stafford Laundry, 123; Stafford Museum, The Green, Stafford, 13, 22, 24, 33, 78, 86, 88, 117, 122; Stafford Photographic Society, 130; Stoke-on-Trent City Museum, Hanley, 63; Mrs Thompson, 19 Station Road, Rugeley, 55; Mr G. J. H. Vincent, The Mackenzie School, Cheadle, 50, 58, 100, 103, 118; Miss K. Wakefield, 1 Sandy Lane, Brewood, 49; Central Library, Lichfield Street, Walsall, 38, 76, 77, 83; Miss L. M. Warham, The Studio, Audley, 51, 84, 138; Miss Weate, Ivetsey Lane, Wheaton Aston, 29, 56, 137; West Midlands Gas Board, Solihull, 111; Trustees of the William Salt Library, Stafford, 23, 105, 125; Mr F. Winfield, C. E. Secondary School, Eccleshall, 1, 21; Trustees of the Wedgwood Museum, Barlaston, 2, 73, 74; Wolverhampton Central Library, 17, 39, 40.

First published 1977
Reprinted 1983, 1985
Text copyright © Pamela Murray and Robert Frost 1977

Phototypeset by Tradespools Ltd, Frome, Somerset
Printed and bound in Great Britain by
Anchor Brendon Ltd, Tiptree, Essex
for the publishers B. T. Batsford Ltd
4 Fitzhardinge Street, London W1H 0AH

ISBN 0 7134 0441 8

CONTENTS

3 Near Rugeley, on Cannock Chase, 1896. Local inhabitants had various common rights on the Chase including the right to collect firewood which is presumably what these ladies had been doing

INTRODUCTION

New or old, Staffordshire as a county is fundamentally 'two-faced'. Sitting on the fence as it does between Midland and Northern England, the divisions in its society run as deep as the divisions in its landscape. The world of the Pennines north of Cheadle – the 'gouty, moorish, peaty, cold black land' of the seventeenth-century historian Robert Plot – is a stark contrast to the riot of hawthorn, bramble and warm red brick of the countryside around Eccleshall. Similarly the division between town and country, industry and agriculture, is deepened, ironically though it may seem, by the fact that the two main old-established industrial areas – the Black Country in the south and the Potteries in the north – kept even into the twentieth century much of the character of urbanised villages rather than centralised towns. Both areas, therefore, retained their individuality together with a strong sense of family and community and their own colourful vocabulary which now and then betrays its country origins.

Our knowledge of these areas and their surroundings in Victorian and Edwardian times can be greatly enhanced by contemporary photographs. The possibility of recording people and places other than by sketches and pictures became available at the beginning of Victoria's reign. In its infancy, photographic equipment was cumbersome; plates often had to be prepared immediately before use and then developed at once. Results were uncertain and only obtained with difficulty. Not unnaturally, early photographers were relatively few in number; yet by 1914 photography had become a mass pastime, its technique within the grasp of many. This change was largely brought about by the introduction of roll films and lightweight cameras in the 1880's, and by advances in lenses and film negatives. By the First World War good quality photography had become possible under most conditions and in most places, and with the greater mobility of the photographer, improved film speeds and better techniques, came spontaneity. The growth of photographic clubs and societies in towns such as Stafford was symptomatic of photography's appeal to amateur and professional alike.

Photographs recreate the atmosphere of the period in a way which print can never do. Unfortunately, though, the sort of things which today would be of greatest interest were not necessarily regarded as worth recording by every photographer or picture postcard publisher of yesterday. Portraits, family groups, important buildings and celebrations abound, but ordinary people at home, at work or relaxing are only too often elusive. Where photographs such as these exist, they show a way of life strangely remote and yet almost attainable. This seeming attainability is perhaps due to the survival of those buildings which have altered little in Staffordshire's towns and villages, but in fact there is less familiarity than curiosity in the strange cars, trains and trams, the shops, the horses, the quieter streets, and the lack of rubbish, which are also revealed. Moreover, the obvious widespread poverty, the occasional archaic tools, the dress and rather serious faces of all classes only tend to emphasise how little we can really hope to know about the totality of their lives. Yet for one fraction of a second their world was frozen on film, thereby enabling us today to see again that which would otherwise be unknown.

Contemporary photographs therefore help clothe the bare bones of facts with atmosphere. In some areas of historical research, indeed, they prove to be the most authoritative source of information available to us. This is particularly true of clothing. Numerous examples of women's 'costume' similar to that worn by Mrs Hollin, the Stafford shoemaker's wife, survive in museums, even occasionally complete with maker's label and a full record of the wearer, but rare indeed are the surviving examples of working people's clothes. The elderly woman standing at her door in Kinver, wearing over her dress a long white apron and a beautifully intricate curtained bonnet; the Pye Green family with their air of working-class respectability; the Maer game-keepers' corduroy suits and the miners outside the Cheadle pub with their caps and mufflers; without photographs such as these the task of the student of working-class costume would be almost hopeless, so few are the examples of working clothing in our museums. This shortage makes for difficulties in dating photographs by costume detail alone. Changes in high fashion, of course, were recorded in magazines and paintings and are therefore reasonably reliable; but the rate of fashion change in a working community was notoriously wayward. For this reason dating by costume alone has been avoided. Wherever possible photographs have been dated exactly from external evidence; where more general dates have had to be used they have been based on the content as a whole and seldom on one aspect alone. The commentaries similarly have been kept factual rather than interpretive, and the photographs allowed to speak for themselves.

How far does the collection of Victorian and Edwardian photographs shown here illustrate the mesh of conflicting energies that is Staffordshire – north and south, agriculture and industry, town and country, rich and poor? The answer is probably very little. We have throughout chosen to show the products and the instigators of environment – people – rather than the environment itself. As such the collection is by no means representative of every industry or town in the county. We are conscious, for example, of the inadequacy of illustrating a complex industry such as shoe-making with a single photograph, and are particularly aware of the lack of material from Leek and Burton. This may be because it has proved for one reason or another more difficult to collect in these towns than elsewhere, but equally many photographs which might have been relevant must have been destroyed or lost. In general, what has survived has done so by pure chance – a housewife consigning a drawerful of albums to the shed rather than to the bonfire. It is equally true that some aspects of Staffordshire life and work which we wished to portray were never recorded on film; they were thought not worth the effort.

Making this collection – much of which remains unpublished – has been a chastening experience, for the total amount of material available proved enormous.

To some extent our final choice was necessarily arbitrary; we have rejected many photographs of poor quality but fascinating content, yet in some areas our choice was so limited that we felt ourselves lucky to find a single representative photograph.

Public collections yielded only a small proportion of the total material available, but as content and reproductive quality were often superior to prints from private sources, libraries, record offices and museums predominate in the final selection. Nevertheless a considerable number of photographs from private individuals, collectors, shops, local newspapers, schools, clubs and public utilities have been included. Even so these are far from exhaustive; at least one large private collection does not figure in this selection. The collecting area covers the geographical rather than the administrative county. Our base is therefore a wide one, and perhaps the special interest of this collection is that many of the photographs which we have selected have never previously been publicly available. Wherever possible, record copies of those prints not in public or large private collections have been deposited at the Staffordshire County Museum, Shugborough.

We would emphasise again, however, that our aim is not to illustrate comprehensively the whole of Staffordshire's topography or economic and social life – more specialised collections will do that much more successfully – but rather to picture Staffordshire people and the quality of their lives before the First World War. For the Staffordshire reader we hope the photographs will conjure up a world that is poignantly familiar from memory or hearsay, but one which is dead and buried nevertheless. Should this familiarity mislead us it is salutory to remember that of the 30 odd firms which are mentioned by name, only a tiny fraction remain in business today.

AT HOME

4 An industrial home with a
backyard family group from Pye
Green, Cannock, in the 1890s

5 Washday in Longnor *c.* 1900.
Mrs Knowles works the dolly peg;
with her are her daughters Edith and
Alice and granddaughters Jessie and
Alice. It was usual to wash outside
whenever the weather allowed

6 The logical conclusion to the use of local stone for house walls: one of Kinver's rock houses, hollowed out of New Red Sandstone. Photograph c. 1895 by Sir Benjamin Stone

7 *Right, above* A terrace of houses in the same outcrop

8 *Right* A Rugeley family celebration: the Christmas pig, 1910. Bacon and fat pork were important in the diet of working people. Nothing was wasted; what could not be salted or eaten immediately was shared among neighbours

TOWNSCAPES

9   Greengate Street, Stafford, looking towards the Ancient High House, *c.* 1860

10   A busy brewing town: Station Street, Burton, *c.* 1905

11 *Top* A mid-Staffordshire brewing and shoe-making town: view down the High Street, Stone on market day, 1910. The Crown Hotel, on the right, remains a feature of the street today

12 *Above* A silk-spinning town of the North Staffordshire moorlands: St Edward Street, Leek, *c*. 1905

13 Stafford, 1910. The timbered building, the seventeenth-century Ancient High House, still stands in the main street as is the bear which marks the Bear Inn on the left

Stafford

A POTTERY TOWN. LONGTON.

14 *Left, above* Piccadilly, Hanley, around 1905. Hanley has an interesting town plan, built around a series of irregular and interlinking squares or triangles. Here we see the top of Piccadilly, looking through to the next square along, Fountain Square

15 *Left* The market square, Hanley, in 1900

16 A Longton landscape at the turn of the century. 'I do not think the Five Towns will ever be described: Dante lived too soon.' – Arnold Bennett in *The Death of Simon Fuge*

17 *Next page* One of the main industrial and service centres for South Staffordshire: Dudley Street, Wolverhampton c. 1900

DEE OIL COMPANY'S
LEUM DEELINÆ
THE SKIN & COMPLEXION
ALVO PETROLIA
PETROLEUM JELLY
AT SHALL I DRINK?
ONTSERRAT
TRADE MARK
FRUIT JUICE
& CORDIALS.
35
DICKINSON
BAKER'S
ENDISH
BATTER
HOSIER
AM & Co
LEEDS
DEWSBURY
CAVENDISH
RESTAURANT
TO THE BAR
AND
WICK
HEMIST

18 *Left* High Street, Uttoxeter, famous for its markets, on a quiet day in 1910. The building next to the Cross Keys Hotel is the Town Hall

19 *Left, below* A small country town – Eccleshall – dressed up for a wedding celebration, *c.* 1900

20 A union march in the Strand, Longton. The building at the far end of the street is The Cricketers' Arms

THE WELL-TO-DO

21 Baby in a bassinet in the care of
her sister and nursemaid, Eccleshall
1900

22 David Hollin, shoe manufacturer,
and wife outside their home at
Highfield Manor, Newport Road,
Stafford. 1905

23　The drawing room at Highfield
Manor

24 The main staircase at Highfield
Manor

25 The music room at Haden Cross
Hall

26 On the terrace at Little Aston Hall, 25 September 1907. The group includes Robert Holder, Mr and Mrs William Derry, William Derry and nurse, and Lady Stone

27 Lucy E. Landor (1816–1898) with her maid Ellen, c. 1895

COUNTRY LIFE

28 Mr Plant, the gardener at Hatherton Hall, *c.* 1900. He is wearing corduroy trousers with a 'front fall' opening, basically an eighteenth-century method of closure but retained long into the nineteenth and even into the twentieth century by working men

29 Tree-fellers from Wheaton Aston near Penkridge at work in Leicestershire shortly before the First World War. Wheaton Aston was the home of a number of such gangs who worked all over the Midlands and Wales. The straight-shafted axe remained their favourite tool until the 1920s

30 A farmer and family: the Fodens of Booth's Farm, Perry Barr in 1900, photographed by Sir Benjamin Stone

31 *Right, above* A shoeing smith's shop at Whiston

32 *Right* A box waggon waiting to be loaded, Hatherton *c.* 1900. Note the ladders fitted to support the hay and the horse's white ear-protectors. Haymaking was an important time both agriculturally and socially as witnessed by the number of photographs showing harvesters at work or relaxing

33 *Left, above* Farmer, farm workers
and contractors with a steam-driven
threshing box, 1910. The farmer could
be Thomas Brindley who farmed near
Hednesford 1900–1912

34 *Left* The Hatherton haymakers at
lunch, *c.* 1900

35 Gamekeepers, probably on the
Maer Hall estate near Ashley, *c.* 1890

PUBLIC SERVICES

36 The head turnkey, Mr J. Chidley, and his family outside their home in the North Tower of Stafford Prison, 1868

37 A Staffordshire police constable and four villains *c.* 1860

39 *Right, above* The kitchen, Wolverhampton workhouse

38 Walsall Petty Sessions Court, 9 November 1896

40 *Right* The women's ward of the workhouse, 1900

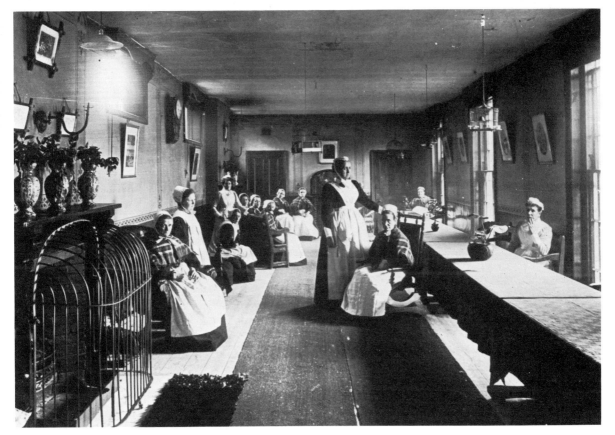

41 *Left* Staff outside the Post Office at Gnosall *c.* 1900

42 *Left, below* Installing the first electric cables in Hanley, 1894. Hanley had the first electricity generating station of all the pottery towns

43 Lamp fitters outside Brookfield's, Stafford

45 *Right, above* Ingestre Fire Engine at work in Great Haywood, 1905. Several engines were brought from surrounding districts to drain a pool into which a motor car had crashed

46 *Right* Mummery's Corner, Market Square, Stafford. Several houses and shops were completely destroyed by a fire which broke out in the Elizabethan House at 1.30 am on 1 October 1887 in spite of the arrival of fire engines from Stone, Ingestre and Rugeley

44 Newcastle Corporation Fire Team in 1894

47 Inside the operating theatre at Stafford Infirmary, 1914

48 Resident almsmen at the Hospital of St John the Baptist, Lichfield in 1900. The origins of the hospital are obscure but it was in existence before 1245; the premises were extended in 1966 and recently supported 17 almsmen

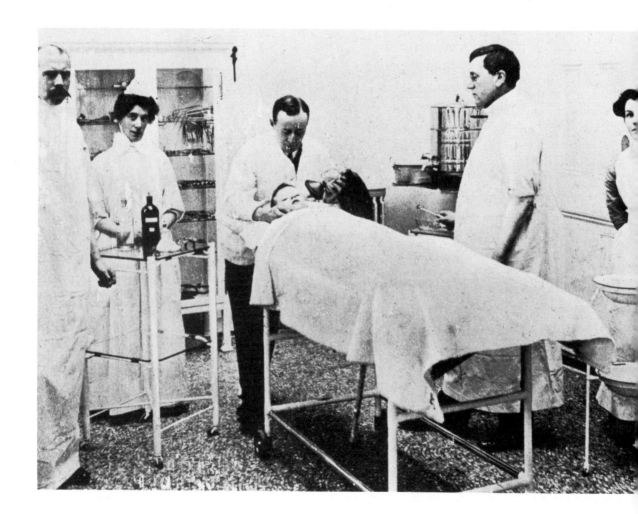

49 Colonel George Singleton Tudor with the First Lapley Volunteers, Staffordshire Yeomanry, at their training camp *c.* 1890

50 Recruits leaving Cheadle railway station for 'The Great War' in 1914, after a tea party given in their honour

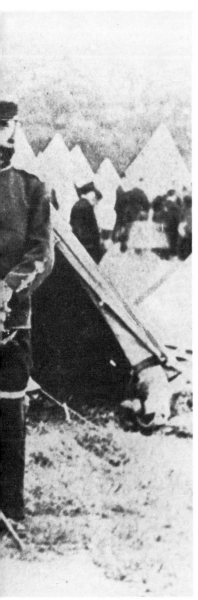

SCHOOL AND CHURCH

51   An art class at Betley Ladies'
College, 1895

52   The gardening class of the Public
Elementary School, Brown Edge,
under the direction of Mr William
Jones. 1913

53 The boys' class of the Royal
School, Wolverhampton (the
'Bluecoats'), *c.* 1900

54 *Right, above* A laundry class at
the Royal School *c.* 1900

55 *Right* Rugeley Church of England
Primary School for Junior Girls,
Standard V, 1913. The school was
founded in 1826 and by 1834 there
were 60 girls paying 2d a week; from
1912 to the 1930s it averaged 230
pupils

56 A class group at Wheaton Aston school *c.* 1910

57 *Left, below* Laying the foundation stone of the Mission Room at the Sytch, Burslem. The mission, which was associated with St Paul's church, was opened in 1894

58 An open-air meeting of the Primitive Methodists at Jimmy's Yard, Oakamoor *c.* 1900. The 'Prims' originated in North Staffordshire

INDUSTRY

Coal Mining

59 The ceremonial re-opening of
New Haden Colliery, Cheadle, 1902

60 The construction of a timber
chock roof support, Baggeridge
Colliery

61 Pit ponies rescued after the
Jammage Colliery, Bignall End, had
been sealed for 21 days after an
explosion on 25 November 1911

62 The coal wharf at Rowley Regis

63 Arnold Bennett, centre, visiting a colliery in Stoke. Marguerite, his French wife, is standing on his left

64 William Potter of Holoway Bank coal jagging near Russell Street, Wednesbury, *c.* 1895. Coal jagging was a local term for the selling of small loads of coal to poorer households straight from the pit

66 Hard times: picking over coal tips in Chesterton, 1910

COAL PICKER — CHESTERTON

67 Wednesbury pit-bank girls, photographed *c*. 1900

68 Children collecting coal in Wharf Street, Longton, probably 1910

The Pottery Industry

69 Throwers' assistants at work in a Longton pottery *c.* 1905

70 *Below* China dipping, Longton, early this century

71 *Opposite page* Bottle kilns at a Longton potbank. The kiln with three fireboxes below is an enamel kiln. Around it are the hovels of three bottle ovens and, left, the engine house chimney. The tall ladder, 'horse', is used for placing saggars inside the oven. The cart is loaded with 'shraff', pottery waste

DIPPING CHINA.

72 *Left* 'Jinneting', removing the uneven marks left by 'stilts' on flatware after glost firing. 'Stilts' and 'spurs' are small supports which separate the goods during firing

73 *Left, below* Flint Mill, part of the Etruria complex, in the 1870s

74 Thomas Lovatt ornamenting a copy of the Portland Vase. Lovatt was one of the most famous decorators to work for Wedgwood's between 1846 and the 1890s

75 Crate-makers at a Longton pottery in the 1870s. Rough stout crates made from hazel wands were the main form of packaging for crocks

ne side of LADIES' BAG DEPT.

Other Industry

76 *Left* The ladies' bag department at Mark Cross, 1910

77 *Right* The case shop at Mark Cross Ltd, Warewell Street, Walsall. The firm began work in the early years of the twentieth century and was flourishing by the time this photograph was taken in 1910

78 The finishing department of Bostock's Shoe Factory, Coton Field, Stafford, 1906. Thomas Bostock began shoemaking in Gaolgate in 1829 and by the mid-1830s had not only taken his son Edwin into partnership in Stafford, but also seen other sons set up business in Stone, and Northampton. In 1903 the Stafford company incorporated Lotus Ltd, a subsidiary company, as a distribution agent. In 1919 all three Bostock factories amalgamated into Lotus

CASE SHOP. Showing Hand Sewing.

79 Sandstone quarrying at Hollington just before the First World War. In the 1830s Hollington was known for its excellent freestone. It is still producing fine quality building stone

80 Crushing sandstone at Gornal early this century. Gornal sandstone has been quarried since the seventeenth century, at first for grindstones and building stone for locks and bridges on the Birmingham canals. The high silica content of the Gornal gritstone led to its nineteenth-century use in firebricks.

81 Women chainmakers at Harry Stevens', Oak Street, Cradley Heath in 1912

82 Chainmakers at Noah Hindley
Ltd in 1910

SPORTS AND PASTIMES

83   The start of a motor cycle rally,
Willenhall, 1911

85 *Left, above* Trentham Park lake, taken near Flood Gate Cottage early this century. The park was a traditional playground for the industrial workers of North Staffordshire

84 Cyclists with penny farthings and bone-shakers at Betley *c.* 1890

86 *Right* An afternoon's fishing at Hopton Pool *c.* 1910

87 A family of pigeon fanciers on the occasion of Cheadle and District Homing Society's seasonal awards 1910. Taken at Back Street, Cheadle, the group includes Mr & Mrs J. Clewlow, Mr B. Knight, Mr E. Clewlow, Mr E. Chandler and Mr & Mrs C. Clewlow

88 *Below* Stafford Rangers football team, 1883

89 Stoke Victoria cricket club, 1863

90 Uttoxeter amateur swimming club *c.* 1905. The club used the river Dove, now considered too dangerous for bathing

ONE VILLAGE

During the nineteenth century and before Longnor was an important
service, market and social centre for the moorland area between Leek and
Buxton. Improved communications gradually robbed the village of this
role which passed to the two nearest towns and even further afield. The
people shown here were photographed just before the First World War

91 The cobbler. The knee clamp
propped up in the corner indicates
that he probably did some saddlery
work too

92 Longnor Village Friendly Club
feast day around 1888. The club was
amalgamated into the Leek and
Moorland Friendly Society in 1918

93   Joshua Millward, Longnor's
auctioneer. Joshua lived at Folds End
Farm and is first registered as
auctioneer in 1872; he was still there
in 1916 but with premises in the
Market Place. By the 1920s Longnor

had neither auctioneer nor cattle
market which had been taken over by
Leek

94   George Slack of Crowdycote,
near Longnor

95 Mr Thomas Smith, a smallholder
from Carder Green. He died during
Wakes Week 1926

MRS HOROBIN, CROWDYCOTE, LONGNOR

97/8 Two views of Mrs Horobin of 'The Meadow', Crowdycote, both sold as postcards in the area. The interior shows her nineteenth-century, blacksmith-made grate, oven and boiler fitted under an older stone hood. The mass-produced iron range was a development of this type of grate

99 Three village characters: left to right, John Barr, saddler, John Finney, postman, George 'Limmer' Wood

TRANSPORT

100   Robert Johnson, known locally as 'Peg Leg' was a signalman. He lost both legs in an accident but continued to work at Bolton's Siding, Froghall

101   Passengers and porters by the bookstall at Stafford station *c.* 1905

102 *Left* Workmen laying track for the North Staffordshire Railway by the entrance to Oakamoor tunnel

103 *Left, below* The first passenger train on the Cresswell to Cheadle line, opened on 1 January 1901. Always mainly a coal line, it closed in 1964

104 Toll gates at Littleworth, Stafford, at the junction of Weston and Tixall Roads. The gates were removed in 1878 and the house pulled down shortly after

106 Richard Howle's steam
furniture removal van (maximum
speed 5 m.p.h.) outside The
Wheatsheaf, Red Street, Chesterton,
c. 1914

105 David Hollin with wife,
daughter and coachman in 1905

107 A steam tram running between
Birmingham and Dudley in 1903

108 At Milford, Cannock Chase
c. 1905. The number ESTA 1 is
unusual. In 1903 Staffordshire was
allocated E but further letters were
not added until much later. It may be
that registration was incorrectly
anticipated and that STA for Stafford
was included with E for the county.
It may well be the first Stafford
registration

109 Kingswinford Motor Service
bus and crew outside the Swan Inn
1912. The bus was a 32 h.p. Albion,
maximum permitted speed 12 m.p.h.

FROGHALL QUARRIES

110   Loading limestone at Froghall on
the Caldon Canal pre-1900. Limestone
was first worked at Caldon Low in the
1770s but the site was abandoned in
1900 and new workings opened
further east, served by rail

111   *Right, above* On 5 September
1862 Henry Coxwell and James
Glashier began a balloon ascent near
Wolverhampton Gas Works. At
29,000 feet Glashier became
unconscious but Coxwell managed to
bring the balloon down near Ludlow.
It had reached 37,000 feet, a record
not broken for 32 years

112   *Right* Grahame White's
aeroplane at Hademore near Lichfield.
On 23 April 1910 White set out to win
the £10,000 offered by the *Daily Mail*
to the first aviator to fly from London
to Manchester in 24 hours with only
two stops. White's engine developed a
fault and he made a forced landing at
Hademore; bad weather prevented
him from continuing

... Mr Grahame White's Aeroplane at Hademore ...

SHOPS AND SERVICES

113   Edward Fryer's general store, St Mary's Place, Stafford, *c.* 1912

114   David Brown, boot dealer and grocer, Dean Street, Brewood. The Browns probably opened up shop 1892–1896 and were still going in 1912

115 Turner & Co, Greengate Street and Martin Place, Stafford, *c.* 1910. The shop specialised in ladies' outfitting and drapery

116 Mrs Ann Pyatt, 94 High Street, Cheadle, probably *c.* 1912. The Pyatts were long-established greengrocers; she seems to have taken over the shop between 1906 and 1912

117 Wigham's Stores, 29 Horse Fair,
Rugeley, 1912

118 David Shenton, printing,
stationery and fancy goods, High
Street, Cheadle, 1900

119 George Mason's, High Street, Dudley, 1900

MASON.

HAMS

121 *Right, above* P. White, dairyman in the Newcastle and Penkhull areas in 1900

122 *Right* R. J. Harris & Son, ironmongers, agricultural and dairy engineers, Market Street, Rugeley, c. 1900

120 Outside The Anchor, Gnosall, 1905

123 The washroom, Stafford
Laundry, 1906

124 Washing hung out to dry at the
back of Stafford Laundry, 1912

125 The cattle market in Gaolgate
Street, Stafford, 1905

126 *Left* The Horse Fair, Rugeley,
early this century. The town has a
long history of livestock fairs, the
earliest charter being granted in 1259.
The horse and colt fair had lapsed by
1940

127 *Left, below* Uttoxeter market,
c. 1911

128 The Butter Cross was the
traditional site of Abbots Bromley's
weekly market, defunct by 50 years
by the time this photograph was taken
in 1899

CELEBRATIONS AND OUTINGS

129   A stop at Lea Grange on the
'Beating of the Bounds' of the city of
Lichfield by the Sheriff, Mayor, Town
Clerk and Corporation, 8 September
1908

130   Stafford Photographic Society on
an outing to Alton, 1907

131 A group of miners outside The Roebuck, Brookhouses, Cheadle, between 1900 and 1908

132 A wedding party, Stafford,
c. 1905

133 Coronation celebrations in
Armitage, June 1911

134 Lichfield children receiving traditional Greenhill Bower Cakes, Whit Monday 1906. The original menu for this Feast was cold hanged beef, stewed prunes, cakes, wine and ale

135 A meeting of Elford Village
Friendly Society 2 June 1903. Squire
Paget is centre

136 *Next page* Abbots Bromley Horn
Dancers, 11 September 1899. The
dance was described by Robert Plot in
The Natural History of Staffordshire,
1686

137 Wheaton Aston Sports Day and Carnival, 1908

138 A bank holiday procession in Church Street, Audley, *c.* 1910

139 Pageant procession in Gaol Square, Stafford *c.* 1910. First prize went to 'Cook by Gas'. Note the splendidly ornate gentlemen's public lavatory to the right of the float

140 Newcastle Wakes, 1905, looking
down Penkhull Street to the Guildhall.
'Roundabouts, swings, switchbacks,
myrioramas, atrocity booths, quack
dentists, shooting galleries, coconut
shies and bazaars . . . The lights, the
colours, the explosions, the shrieks,
the statuary, the August night and the
mingling of a thousand melodies in a
counterpoint beyond the dreams of
Wagner.' Arnold Bennett in *'The Dog'*